LUSCIOUS & CREAMY DESSERT CLASSICS

CONTENTS

Luscious & Creamy Dessert Classics

People of all nations and cultures adore smooth, scrumptious sweets. Here's a roundup of irresistible offerings from five main regions of the world.

The Mediterranean

If it's a special occasion here, there's bound to be a lavish dessert on the menu. The Italians, especially, are known for their exquisite creations—cakes, iced treats, and luxurious custards. Many creamy concoctions, such as tiramisu, are enhanced with coffee and fine liqueurs.

Latin America & the Caribbean

A touch of the exotic is a characteristic of the desserts found here. Often featured are coconuts and fresh fruits, such as bananas and pineapples. Popular flavors include vanilla, cinnamon, and ginger.

Northern & Eastern Europe

Delicate cream desserts are the sweet finales of many festive European meals. At one time, these treats graced only the tables of the wealthy, who were able to afford the large quantities of sugar required to make them. Upon the introduction of the sugar beet, sweets became affordable to

NORTH AMERICA & AUSTRALIA

You don't have to be a kid to love the playful confections that are so popular in these regions. Cotton candy and ice cream are perennial crowd-pleasers, but more refined creations—like soft chocolate soufflés and airy mousses—are also widely enjoyed. American and Australian bakers know that generous amounts of butter, chocolate, eggs, cream, and other rich ingredients are essential to making the finest cakes, puddings, and custards.

ASIA

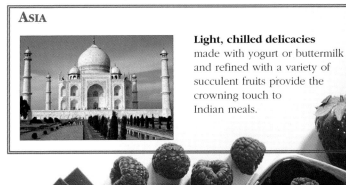

Light, chilled delicacies made with yogurt or buttermilk and refined with a variety of succulent fruits provide the crowning touch to Indian meals.

everyone. Soon, delicious desserts with such melodious names as Bavarian Cream, Charlotte Russe, and Mousse au Chocolat became widely coveted and imitated. Original versions of these favorite treats—as well as many new and creative variations—are savored to this day.

TEMPTING TIRAMISU

ITALY

This irresistible Italian dessert has become a worldwide favorite. Rich, creamy mascarpone gives the treat its velvety texture, while coffee and Marsala lend aromatic accents.

INGREDIENTS
(Serves 6)

- 3 large egg yolks
- 3 tablespoons sugar
- 2 cups Mascarpone cheese
- 2 teaspoons grated lemon peel
- ¾ cup espresso or very strong coffee
- ¼ cup Marsala or sherry
- 15 crisp ladyfinger cookies

IN ADDITION
- 1 tablespoon cocoa powder as garnish

INGREDIENT TIP
You can find mascarpone, the luscious soft Italian cream cheese, at some supermarkets. Or you can substitute ¾ cup of any soft cream cheese lightened with ½ cup whipped cream.

1 In a large bowl suspended over a pan of gently simmering water, whisk the yolks, sugar, and 4 tablespoons water for about 3 minutes, until thick, pale yellow, and hot (about 140°F). Remove from over water.

2 Whisk the mascarpone into the egg mixture a little at a time until smooth. Whisk in the lemon peel.

Step 2

3 In a shallow dish, mix together the espresso and Marsala. Quickly dip the ladyfingers into the espresso mixture. Line the bottom of an 8 x 8-inch glass dish with half the ladyfingers, cutting them to fit if necessary.

Step 3

4 Spread half of the mascarpone cream over the ladyfingers. Repeat the layering with the remaining ladyfingers and mascarpone. Cover and refrigerate for at least 3 hours.

5 Sprinkle a thick layer of cocoa powder over the tiramisu through a small sieve before serving.

Step 4

Preparation: 30 minutes
Chilling: 3 hours
Per serving: 519 cal; 10 g pro; 40 g fat; 27 g carb.

TYPICALLY ITALIAN
In the beautiful, hilly Italian countryside—and far beyond Italy's borders—tiramisu is a much-adored dessert. The English translation of tiramisu is "pick me up," and the strong espresso in this layered specialty certainly does give it a kick.

COOKING TIP

As a substitute for Marsala or sherry, you can use brandy, coffee liqueur, or a combination of the two. Any of these spirits will add complexity to the flavor of the dessert.

SERVING TIPS

Tiramisu is also lovely served in individual portions. Just crumble the ladyfingers into dessert dishes, sprinkle with espresso, and fill with the cream. A small glass of amaretto and a cappuccino are perfect accompaniments.

ℐCE CREAM BOMBE

ITALY

This enchanting treat, known as zuccotto, is well worth the effort. The dome of cake slices encloses a delicious surprise—chocolate and vanilla ice cream accented with orange flavor.

INGREDIENTS

(Serves 12)

FOR THE CAKE

- 5 large eggs, separated
- ½ cup sugar
- ⅔ cup all-purpose flour
- ¼ cup cocoa powder
- ¾ cup apricot jam, warmed until spreadable

FOR THE FILLING

- 1 pint chocolate ice cream
- 1 pint vanilla ice cream
- 2 tablespoons orange liqueur
- 2 tablespoons minced candied orange peel

IN ADDITION

- strawberries and whipped cream as garnish

INGREDIENT TIP

If you wish, try using other flavors of ice cream, such as chocolate chip or mocha.

1 Preheat the oven to 400°F. Line a jelly-roll pan with wax paper. Beat the egg yolks, sugar, and 5 tablespoons water with an electric mixer until thick and pale, about 5 minutes. Beat the egg whites until stiff and fold into the yolks. Sift the flour and cocoa over the eggs; gently fold in. Evenly spread the batter in the pan and bake for 10 minutes.

Step 1

2 Dust a kitchen towel with sugar. Invert the cake onto the towel immediately after baking and remove the paper. Spread the jam evenly onto the cake. Roll it up and let cool, seam side down, for 1 hour.

Step 2

3 Line a dome-shaped 1½ quart bowl with plastic wrap. Cut the cake into 18 slices and line the bowl with 12 of them.

4 Let the ice cream soften briefly. Spread the chocolate ice cream over the cake in the bowl, leaving a well. Mix the liqueur and orange peel into the vanilla ice cream; pour into the well. Top with 6 jelly-roll slices. Cover and freeze for 3 hours until firm.

Step 4

5 Invert the bombe onto a serving dish and remove the plastic. Garnish with strawberries and whipped cream.

Preparation: 1 hour
Cooking: 10 minutes
Cooling and freezing: 4 hours
Per serving: 250 cal; 5 g pro;
7 g fat; 42 g carb.

TYPICALLY TUSCAN

Large ice cream bombes and cakes are popular all over Italy. Some say the shape of this spectacular dessert was inspired by Florence's famous Duomo, the cathedral of Santa Maria del Fiore.

COOKING TIPS

When rolling up the cake, hold the towel firmly at one end and carefully pull upward. This will work best when the cake is still hot.

The jelly roll can be prepared the day before. If you wrap it in plastic, it will stay fresh and moist.

SERVING TIP

Decorating the bombe with stripes of whipped cream can turn it into a little work of art. If you wish, you can cover it beforehand with a dark chocolate glaze, then decorate.

SERVING TIPS Paper-thin, twisted lime slices make highly decorative touches for this dessert.

Freshly squeezed orange juice or a glass of Marsala are both pleasing beverage accompaniments.

ℒEMON-LIME CREAM

This fluffy cream has a delightful tangy-sweet flavor. It's an easy-to-make recipe for any time of year—and a perfect refresher after a robust Italian repast.

INGREDIENTS
(Serves 4)

- ½ package unflavored gelatin
- 2 limes
- 1 lemon
- ½ cup plus 2 tablespoons sugar
- 2 large eggs
- pinch of cream of tartar
- 1 cup heavy cream

IN ADDITION

- 1 lime, sliced
- peel of 1 lemon, cut into thin strips

INGREDIENT TIP

When cooking with lemons and limes, it's always best to grate the peels before cutting the fruit in half for juicing.

1 Soften the gelatin in 2 tablespoons cold water for 5 minutes. Grate the peels from the limes and lemon, and squeeze the juice.

2 Heat the juice and grated peel in a small saucepan, but do not boil. Remove from the heat. Add the gelatin and ½ cup of the sugar and stir until dissolved.

Step 1

3 Separate the eggs. Beat the yolks and 1 tablespoon sugar in the top of a double boiler over simmering water for 3 minutes, until thick and pale. Add the gelatin mixture; beat until creamy. Cover and refrigerate until the mixture begins to set, about 15 minutes.

Step 3

4 In the top of a clean double boiler over simmering water, beat the egg whites with 1 tablespoon water, the remaining 1 tablespoon sugar, and the cream of tartar until stiff. In another bowl, whip the cream until stiff. Gently fold the whites into the cream, then fold into lemon-lime mixture.

Step 4

5 Divide the cream among 4 bowls. Cover and refrigerate for 1 hour. Garnish the dessert with lime slices and lemon-peel strips before serving.

Preparation: 45 minutes
Chilling: 1 hour
Per serving: 376 cal; 5 g pro; 25 g fat; 36 g carb.

TYPICALLY SICILIAN

Open markets teeming with fresh, colorful fruits and vegetables lure passersby in the streets of Sicily's towns and villages. Locally grown citrus fruits are of excellent quality, making ideal additions to creamy desserts.

PANNA COTTA WITH BLACKBERRY SAUCE

ITALY

Panna Cotta—which means "cooked cream"—is a luscious custard from Italy. Here, the dessert is flavored with vanilla and served with a blackberry puree and toasted pistachios.

INGREDIENTS
(Serves 5)

- 1 vanilla bean
- 1¼ cups heavy cream
- ¾ cup milk
- ¼ cup sugar
- 1 package unflavored gelatin

FOR THE PUREE

- 1½ cups blackberries
- 2 tablespoons confectioners' sugar
- 1 tablespoon grappa

IN ADDITION

- toasted pistachio nuts

INGREDIENT TIPS

- If you like, substitute a fruit brandy for grappa, or simply omit it.
- Frozen berries are a fine substitute for the fresh ones.

1 Split the vanilla bean lengthwise and scrape out the pulp. Mix the bean, pulp, cream, milk, and sugar in a saucepan.

2 Let the cream mixture simmer gently for 15 minutes. Meanwhile, soften the gelatin in ¼ cup cold water for 5 minutes.

3 Remove the vanilla bean from the hot-cream mixture. Add the gelatin and stir until it dissolves.

4 Pour the cream into five 6-ounce molds that have been rinsed with cold water. Cover the molds with plastic wrap and refrigerate for about 3 hours, until set.

5 Wash and sort the blackberries, putting aside a few for garnish. Puree the remaining berries in the food processor, then press through a sieve and mix with the confectioners' sugar and grappa.

6 Spoon the puree onto 5 dessert plates, unmold the panna cotta and place on the plates. Garnish with blackberries and pistachio nuts.

Step 1

Step 5

Step 6

Preparation: 30 minutes
Chilling: 3 hours
Per serving: 312 cal; 4 g pro; 23 g fat; 22 g carb.

TYPICALLY ITALIAN

Grappa, the high-proof spirit from Northern Italy, has gained in popularity in recent years. Distilled from the crushed grapes left in the press after the removal of juice for wine-making, grappa is enjoyed as an after-dinner *digestif* or used in desserts.

COOKING TIPS
• The blackberry puree is passed through a fine sieve in order to remove even the smallest seeds.
• To unmold the custard, loosen the rim carefully with a knife. Briefly wrapping a wet, hot towel around the mold also makes the job easier.

SERVING TIP
Try panna cotta with caramel: Coat the molds with hot caramelized sugar, chill until hardened, then pour in the cream. Cover, chill overnight, and unmold before serving. Garnish with orange-peel slivers.

ICE CREAM DESSERTS—THREE WAYS

Creamy vanilla ice cream combined with cappuccino, strawberries, or bananas make deliciously cool summer pleasers.

BASIC VANILLA ICE CREAM

Vanilla ice cream is ever so easy to make—and calls for only a few ingredients.

(SERVES 4)
- 2 cups heavy cream
- 4 egg yolks
- ¼ cup sugar
- 2 teaspoons vanilla extract

1 In a saucepan, bring the cream to a boil; remove from the heat.

2 Whisk the yolks and sugar until thick and pale. Whisk a little hot cream into the yolks; whisk the yolk mixture into the saucepan. Cook over low heat, stirring, for 5 minutes, until the mixture coats a spoon. Strain, let cool, and add the vanilla. Freeze in an ice cream maker according to the manufacturer's instructions.

CAPPUCCINO-ALMOND PARFAITS

Preparation: 30 Minutes   Freezing: 4 Hours

ITALY

- Basic Vanilla Ice Cream

IN ADDITION
- 2 teaspoons instant espresso powder
- 2 tablespoons honey
- ½ cup heavy cream
- 1 tablespoon confectioners' sugar
- drop of almond extract
- 2 tablespoons almond slices

3 Dissolve the espresso powder in 3 tablespoons hot water. Heat the honey over low heat for 2 minutes. Mix in the espresso and 1 tablespoon cream.

4 Whip remaining cream, sugar, and almond extract. Scoop ice cream into bowls; drizzle with espresso sauce. Top with whipped cream and almonds.

TROPICAL FUDGE SUNDAES

Preparation: 30 minutes   Freezing: 4 hours

DOMINICAN REPUBLIC

- Basic Vanilla
  Ice Cream

  IN ADDITION
- 4 ounces semi-
  sweet chocolate
- $1\frac{1}{2}$ cups heavy
  cream
- 2 tablespoons rum
- $\frac{1}{2}$ teaspoon
  cinnamon
- 2 ripe bananas
- $\frac{1}{4}$ cup shredded
  coconut, toasted
- waffle cookies

3 Finely chop the chocolate. Bring 1 cup of the cream to a boil. Add the chocolate, rum, and cinnamon and reduce the heat to low. Stir until the mixture is smooth. Let cool. Beat the remaining $\frac{1}{2}$ cup cream until stiff. Slice the bananas.

4 Scoop the ice cream into bowls and top with the bananas, chocolate sauce, whipped cream and toasted coconut. Garnish with the waffle cookies.

STRAWBERRY-LEMON CUPS

Preparation: 30 minutes   Freezing: 4 hours

RUSSIA

- Basic Vanilla
  Ice Cream

  IN ADDITION
- 1 pint strawberries
- 1 lemon
- $\frac{1}{2}$ cup heavy cream
- 1 tablespoon
  confectioners' sugar

3 Hull and quarter the strawberries. Grate and juice the lemon.

4 Whip the cream with the sugar until thick but not stiff. Fold in $\frac{1}{2}$ teaspoon lemon juice and 1 teaspoon lemon peel.

5 Scoop ice cream into bowls and top with the strawberries. Drizzle the lemon cream on top.

ℱRUITED SWISS PARFAITS

SWITZERLAND

INGREDIENTS
(Serves 4)

- 1 pint strawberries
- 2 tablespoons granulated sugar
- 1 tablespoon confectioners' sugar
- 1 tablespoon honey
- ½ teaspoon vanilla extract
- 1 small lemon

FOR THE PARFAIT
- 1⅓ cups vanilla frozen yogurt

IN ADDITION
- ½ cup heavy cream
- 2 tablespoons chopped walnuts

INGREDIENT TIP

Instead of vanilla frozen yogurt, try different flavors, such as strawberry, peach, or chocolate.

Layers of fresh strawberries and a semifrozen yogurt cream make a scrumptious ending to any meal. For a pretty accent, finish with a swirl of whipped cream and chopped walnuts.

1 Wash the strawberries and pat dry. Select 4 nice ones and set them aside for garnish. Hull the rest of the berries and cut them into halves or quarters, depending on their size.

2 In a large bowl, whisk together the granulated sugar, confectioners' sugar, honey, and vanilla until smooth.

Step 2

3 Wash and dry the lemon. Finely grate the peel and squeeze the juice. Stir the peel and juice into the honey mixture. Add the strawberries and stir them in gently. Cover and refrigerate for 2–3 hours.

Step 3

4 Divide half the strawberries among 4 parfait glasses. Top with the yogurt, then with the remaining berries. Spoon any leftover strawberry liquid over the parfaits.

5 Beat the heavy cream until stiff. Transfer the cream to a pastry bag fitted with a star tip and pipe the cream decoratively on top of the parfaits. Garnish with the chopped walnuts and the reserved whole strawberries.

Step 5

Preparation: 30 minutes
Chilling: 2–3 hours
Per serving: 262 cal; 4 g pro; 15 g fat; 32 g carb.

TYPICALLY SWISS
The Swiss value tradition and often seek to preserve beautiful customs. In some regions, milk is still brought in cans by horse and wagon from farm to market.

COOKING TIP

Be careful when stirring the strawberries into the honey mixture. Try to coat the berries with the liquid without mashing or breaking them apart.

SERVING TIPS

This strawberry parfait makes a wonderful dessert for a Champagne brunch or luncheon. Start with canapés—bite-size sandwiches with smoked salmon, cheese, and ham. Serve a chilled Champagne or Prosecco.

$\mathcal{F}$LUFFY CHOCOLATE MOUSSE

FRANCE

This heavenly whipped chocolate dessert lends a crowning touch to any feast. And it can be made hours in advance, leaving almost no last-minute work for the cook.

INGREDIENTS
(Serves 4)

- 4 ounces semisweet chocolate
- 3½ tablespoons butter
- 2 large eggs plus 3 egg whites
- 2 tablespoons sugar
- ¼ teaspoon cream of tartar

IN ADDITION
- grated white chocolate

INGREDIENT TIPS
- To be sure the eggs are fresh, you should use them within three weeks of the date on the carton.
- For this dessert, splurge on the best-quality chocolate you can find—it can make all the difference!

1 In the top of a double boiler over simmering water, melt the chocolate and butter, stirring until smooth.

2 Separate the eggs. Place the yolks and 1 tablespoon sugar in the top of a clean double boiler over simmering water and whisk for 5 minutes, until thick and pale. Beat in the chocolate mixture. Let cool.

3 In the top of a clean double boiler over simmering water, beat the egg whites, cream of tartar, and 3 tablespoons water with an electric mixer for 3 minutes, or until foamy. Add the remaining 1 tablespoon sugar and beat until stiff but not dry, about 5 minutes.

4 Fold the egg whites gently into the chocolate mixture. Transfer the mousse to a bowl and refrigerate for at least 3 hours.

5 To serve, spoon out dollops of the mousse and sprinkle with the grated white chocolate.

Step 1

Step 4

Step 5

Preparation: 40 minutes
Chilling: 3 hours
Per serving: 299 cal; 7 g pro; 21 g fat; 25 g carb.

TYPICALLY FRENCH
Chocolate mousse is one of the most passionately loved desserts in France and many other countries. It's sure to be found among the sweet offerings at authentic French bistros and cafes.

COOKING TIP

Instead of washing out the double boiler three times for this recipe, you can create a makeshift double boiler by placing a metal mixing bowl over a saucepan of simmering water. Just make sure to handle the bowl with a pot holder, since it can get quite hot.

SERVING TIPS

Powdered sugar, chopped pistachios, and mint sprigs can also be used as garnishes for the mousse. A cup of strong French-roast coffee is the ideal accompaniment here.

ALSATIAN RASPBERRY SOUFFLÉS

FRANCE

These pretty pink soufflés are chilled—which is ideal when you need to have dessert ready ahead of time. As a special touch, they're topped with whipped cream swirls and fresh berries.

INGREDIENTS

(Serves 4)

- 1½ cups raspberries
- 1 lemon
- 5 tablespoons sugar
- 1 packet unflavored gelatin
- 2 large eggs, separated
- ⅔ cup sour cream
- 2 tablespoons frozen orange juice concentrate
- pinch of cream of tartar

IN ADDITION

- ¼ cup heavy cream, whipped and sweetened

INGREDIENT TIP

If you prefer, substitute an equal amount of frozen raspberries for the fresh. Just make sure to let them thaw before using.

1 Set aside ½ cup raspberries. Grate the peel and squeeze the lemon. Mix with remaining berries and 1 tablespoon sugar.

2 Sprinkle the gelatin over ¼ cup water in a small saucepan; let soften for 5 minutes. In a double boiler over simmering water, whisk the yolks with 2 tablespoons sugar and 2 tablespoons water for 5 minutes, until thick. Remove the bowl from the hot water; stir in sour cream and orange juice.

3 Press the raspberries through a sieve into the yolk mixture. Warm the bowl of gelatin over low heat, stirring until the gelatin dissolves; stir into the berry mixture.

4 In a clean double boiler, beat the whites, cream of tartar, 1 teaspoon water, and remaining 2 tablespoons sugar with a mixer for 5 minutes. Fold into the berry cream.

5 Make collars around four 6-ounce ramekins with 4 wide foil strips folded in half. Divide the berry cream among the dishes; refrigerate for 2 hours. To serve, remove the foil. Scrape the whipped cream into a pastry bag; pipe rosettes on the soufflés. Garnish with the reserved berries.

Step 2

Step 3

Step 5

Preparation: 45 minutes
Chilling: 2 hours
Per serving: 289 cal; 7 g pro; 16 g fat; 31 g carb.

TYPICALLY ALSATIAN

The Alsace region of northeastern France is a gourmet's paradise. In *Guide Michelin*, the famous French restaurant guide, Alsatian eateries rank high for their exquisite cuisine.

COOKING TIPS

• In order to guarantee lump-free gelatin, mix some
of the fruit cream with the dissolved gelatin, then stir
this mixture slowly into the rest of the fruit cream.

   After removing the aluminum foil (Step 5), use a
knife that has been dipped in hot water to smooth
the edges around each soufflé.

SERVING TIP

You can also prepare this dessert
in a large mold and scoop it out.
Spoon a decorative pattern of white
and dark chocolate sauce onto the dessert
dishes. Arrange the scoops on the dishes and
garnish with raspberries.

CLASSIC CRÈME BRÛLÉE

FRANCE

This pale yellow, vanilla-scented custard, glazed with a golden crust of caramelized sugar, is a French specialty. Its sublime flavor and consistency never fail to enchant.

INGREDIENTS
(Serves 6)

- 2 vanilla beans
- 1¼ cups heavy cream
- pinch of salt
- 2 large eggs plus 2 yolks
- 2 tablespoons sugar

FOR THE CARAMEL
- 3 tablespoons sugar

INGREDIENT TIP

For a variation with fewer calories, substitute whole milk for the heavy cream. Do not use skim milk, however, since milk fat is a necessary conveyer of flavor.

1 Preheat the oven to 350°F. Fill a flat-bottomed roasting pan with 1½ inches of hot water; place in the center of the oven.

2 Split the vanilla beans and scrape out the pulp. Place the beans, pulp, cream, and salt in a saucepan; bring to a simmer.

Step 2

3 In a bowl, beat together the eggs, yolks, and 2 tablespoons sugar until light and slightly thickened. Whisk in the hot cream in a fine stream. Remove the beans.

Step 3

4 Pour the mixture into six 4-ounce ramekins. Place these in the prepared roasting pan. Bake until just set and slightly wobbly in the center, 15–20 minutes. Remove the molds from the water; let cool completely on a rack. Cover and refrigerate for 3 hours or overnight.

5 Heat the broiler. Sprinkle the remaining 3 tablespoons sugar over the custards. Place on a baking sheet or in a roasting pan, then place under the broiler and cook until caramelized, 1–3 minutes. Let cool before serving.

Step 4

Preparation: 25 minutes
Baking: 20 minutes
Chilling: 3 hours
Per serving: 256 cal; 4 g pro; 22 g fat; 12 g carb.

TYPICALLY PARISIAN
Since its invention, crème brûlée has become a standard menu entry in the elegant Parisian restaurants where "haute cuisine" was cultivated. Today it is among the best-loved desserts throughout France and many other parts of the world.

COOKING TIP

It's easy to make this dessert's similarly famous sibling, crème caramel: Melt $3\frac{1}{2}$ tablespoons sugar in a saucepan until it's golden yellow, pour into the molds, then pour the cream mixture on top. After cooking the custards in the water bath, let them cool in their molds, then invert onto plates to unmold.

SERVING TIPS

Offer a delicate pâté with salad as an hors d'oeuvre, then roast chicken with asparagus as a main dish. Conclude with the crème brûlée for a typical Parisian menu. A fine sweet white wine, such as Sauternes, rounds out the feast.

STRAWBERRY SWIRL

FRANCE

Here's an irresistible French treat that'll melt in your mouth. Smooth vanilla cream and a tangy strawberry puree are swirled together in this elegantly colorful dessert.

INGREDIENTS
(Serves 4)

- 1 package unflavored gelatin
- 1 vanilla bean
- 1 cup milk
- 4 large egg yolks
- ⅔ cup confectioners' sugar
- 1 cup heavy cream
- ½ pint strawberries

IN ADDITION

- 8 strawberries, quartered
- mint sprigs for garnish
- whipped cream for garnish

INGREDIENT TIPS

- You can also make the mousse with raspberries, blackberries, or a colorful wild-berry mixture. If you prefer, use frozen berries.
- For garnishing, use peppermint, which is sold at produce markets. It will stay fresh in the refrigerator for a day or two.

1 In a small bowl, sprinkle the gelatin over ¼ cup water. Set aside to soften for 5 minutes. Split the vanilla bean lengthwise and scrape out the pulp. Place the bean, pulp, milk, and softened gelatin in a small saucepan; bring to a simmer.

2 Meanwhile, in a double boiler over simmering water, beat the yolks and sugar until light, hot, and frothy, about 5 minutes. Remove the yolk mixture from the heat; whisk in the hot-milk mixture.

3 Let the custard cool to room temperature, then refrigerate until cold and beginning to gel, about 1 hour. Beat the cream just until it holds a soft shape; fold into the egg mixture.

4 Hull then puree the strawberries. Place the puree in a medium bowl. Add half of the vanilla cream; fold gently to blend.

5 In a serving bowl, place the remaining half of the vanilla cream. Scrape the strawberry cream on top and swirl to marbleize. Cover and refrigerate for 3 hours, until set. Garnish with the strawberry quarters, mint, and whipped cream.

Step 1

Step 4

Step 5

Preparation: 30 minutes
Cooling and chilling: 4 hours
Per serving: 415 cal; 11 g pro; 29 g fat; 28 g carb.

TYPICALLY BRETON
Wonderfully fragrant strawberries thrive in Bretagne (or Brittany), a region in the extreme west of France. Large quantities of these delicious berries appear in the local markets in May and June.

COOKING TIPS

• If the berries are cold, slightly heat the fruit puree before blending in the vanilla cream to avoid lumping.
• To make the prettiest marbleized effect, be careful not to overmix the two creams (Step 5). For best results, drag a narrow spatula or wooden spoon handle through the layered cream a few times.

SERVING TIP

For an excellent light meal before this strawberry mousse, serve fillet of sole in a white wine and parsley sauce, along with a mixed salad, French bread, and a glass of Chardonnay.

SERVING TIP Here's a delicious alternative: Spread the rhubarb and strawberry cream on pancakes or crepes, roll them up, then serve with a simple strawberry puree. Garnish with whole fruits.

ℛHUBARB-STRAWBERRY TREAT

GERMANY

Here's a wonderful dessert that features a classic springtime pairing—strawberries and rhubarb. It's a vibrant finale to spring and summer suppers.

INGREDIENTS
(Serves 4)

FOR THE COMPOTE
- ¾ pound rhubarb
- ½ cup orange juice
- ⅓ cup sugar
- ½ teaspoon cinnamon
- 1 teaspoon cornstarch

FOR THE CREAM
- 1 cup ricotta cheese
- 1 tablespoon sugar
- 1 teaspoon vanilla extract
- ½ cup heavy cream

IN ADDITION
- ½ pint strawberries

INGREDIENT TIP

For a dessert light in both fat and calories, use part-skim ricotta cheese instead of the whole-milk variety.

1 Wash and clean the rhubarb. Remove the leaves and carefully peel the stems. Cut the stalks into ½-inch pieces.

2 Put the rhubarb, orange juice, sugar, and cinnamon into a saucepan. Bring to a boil, then lower the heat and simmer, covered, until the rhubarb is tender, about 5 minutes.

Step 1

3 In a small bowl, mix the cornstarch with 1 tablespoon cold water; add this to the rhubarb and bring it to a boil again. Remove from the heat and let cool for 1 hour.

4 For the cream, whisk together the ricotta cheese with the sugar and vanilla until smooth. Beat the heavy cream until stiff and fold it gently into the ricotta mixture.

Step 2

5 Wash the strawberries and reserve 4 of them. Halve the remaining berries and fold into the rhubarb compote along with the ricotta mixture. Divide the cream among 4 tall dessert glasses and refrigerate for 1 hour. Garnish each dessert with a strawberry before serving.

Step 5

Preparation: 35 minutes
Cooling and chilling: 2 hours
Per serving: 334 cal; 9 g pro;
19 g fat; 33 g carb.

TYPICALLY GERMAN
Locally grown fresh rhubarb appears in German markets in April. Until its season comes to an end in July, rhubarb is heartily enjoyed in sauces, chutneys, jellies, salads, baked goods—and of course, desserts.

VANILLA BAVARIAN CREAM WITH RASPBERRY SAUCE

GERMANY

An all-time favorite dessert is given a new twist here—it's served semifrozen and drizzled with a warm raspberry puree. Tangy, cool, and velvety-smooth, it's sure to please.

INGREDIENTS
(Serves 4-6)

- 1 package unflavored gelatin
- 1 cup milk
- 4 large egg yolks
- ⅓ cup granulated sugar
- 2 teaspoons vanilla extract
- 1 cup heavy cream

FOR THE PUREE
- 1½ cups raspberries
- 3 tablespoons confectioners' sugar

INGREDIENT TIP

This dessert can be flavored in many different ways: Add 3½ ounces of ground roasted hazelnuts with the whipped cream. Or mix 1 tablespoon finely grated citrus peel or ½ tablespoon instant coffee to the milk in Step 1.

1 In a small bowl, sprinkle the gelatin over 2 tablespoons cold water; let soften for 5 minutes. Bring the milk to a simmer in a small saucepan.

2 Meanwhile, in a large bowl, whisk the egg yolks and granulated sugar until light in color. Gradually whisk in the hot milk, then place the bowl over a pot with 1 inch of simmering water. Cook, stirring, until the mixture is hot and thick enough to coat the back of a spoon, about 5 minutes. Remove from heat; stir in the gelatin and vanilla. Let cool, whisking occasionally.

3 Refrigerate the yolk mixture until cold and beginning to gel. Beat the cream until barely stiff, then fold into the egg mixture. Scrape into a 4-cup dessert mold. Freeze for 3 hours.

4 Reserve ¼ cup raspberries; press the remainder through a sieve into a saucepan. Add the confectioners' sugar; place over low heat to warm through.

5 Unmold Bavarian onto a serving platter. Spoon the puree and reserved berries on top. Cut into wedges and serve.

Step 2

Step 4

Step 5

Preparation: 50 minutes
Freezing: 3 hours
Per serving: 338 cal; 6 g pro; 24 g fat; 26 g carb.

TYPICALLY BAVARIAN
Bavarian cream made its entry into international cuisine with the French name *fromage bavaroise*. Some believe this silky dessert was created by the renowned French chef Antonin Carême for a visiting Bavarian dignitary.

COOKING TIP

It's easy to unmold this Bavarian—and other molded desserts. Soak a kitchen towel in hot tap water, carefully ring out excess water, then wrap around the mold. Let rest for 1 minute; run a knife around the inside of the form. Invert a platter on top, flip, and remove the container. Repeat if necessary.

SERVING TIP

Make it pretty: Pour raspberry sauce onto a dish and place a spoonful of partially whipped cream in the middle. With a spoon handle, swirl the whipped cream into the sauce for a decorative effect; unmold the dessert onto the center of the dish.

DUTCH VANILLA DELIGHT

THE NETHERLANDS

INGREDIENTS

(Serves 4)

FOR THE CREAM

- 1½ tablespoons unflavored gelatin (1½ packages)
- ½ orange
- 1 cup yogurt
- ¼ cup granulated sugar
- 1 teaspoon vanilla extract
- 2 large egg whites
- pinch of cream of tartar
- ½ cup heavy cream

FOR THE PUREE & GARNISH

- 3 cups black currants or blackberries
- 2 tablespoons crème de cassis
- 1 tablespoon confectioners' sugar
- currants and mint sprigs

INGREDIENT TIP

If you like, you can replace crème de cassis, the black currant liqueur, with orange liqueur or orange juice.

Here's a simple pleasure from Holland—smooth, wholesome yogurt flavored with zesty orange and topped with a delicately tart black-currant sauce.

1 In a small saucepan, sprinkle the gelatin over ⅓ cup cold water; set aside to soften for 5 minutes. Finely grate the orange peel and squeeze out the juice.

2 In a bowl, whisk the yogurt, 2 tablespoons granulated sugar, the vanilla, orange juice, and peel. Place the pan of gelatin over low heat; stir until dissolved. Whisk into yogurt one drop at a time.

Step 2

3 Over simmering water, whisk the egg whites, cream of tartar, remaining 2 tablespoons sugar, and 1 teaspoon water. Beat for 3 minutes, until hot and fluffy. Remove from the heat; let cool. Whip the cream until stiff. Fold the cream, then egg whites into the yogurt. Scrape into a 8 x 4-inch loaf pan. Cover; refrigerate for 2 hours.

Step 4

4 Strip the currants off the stem with a fork. Press through a sieve. Stir in the crème de cassis and confectioners' sugar.

5 To serve, cut around the cream with a knife to release from the pan. Invert onto a plate to unmold. Cut into 4 servings. Place on dessert plates and garnish with the currant puree, currants, and mint.

Step 5

Preparation: 50 minutes,
Chilling: 2 hours
Per serving: 297 cal; 8 g pro;
12 g fat, 37 g carb.

TYPICALLY DUTCH

The serene grazing pastures and dairies of Holland make it one of the world's biggest producers of cheese, cream, and yogurt. Chef and home cooks use these farm-fresh goods to make both sweet and savory fare.

COOKING TIPS

• Fold the whipped cream and egg white gently into the yogurt cream. Do not stir vigorously or you will deplete the air that was whipped into them.

The currant sauce can be prepared and refrigerated two to three days before serving.

SERVING TIP

Dark iced coffee with fresh whipped cream and Dutch shortbread cookies are wonderful accompaniments to this airy, delectable dessert.

ℬLACK-AND-WHITE MOUSSE CAKE

GREAT BRITAIN

This terrifically decadent dessert features fluffy white chocolate mousse layered atop dark semisweet chocolate mousse. Enjoy it as the British do—with a cup of tea.

INGREDIENTS
(Serves 8)

- 4 ounces semisweet chocolate
- 4 ounces white chocolate
- 4 large eggs, separated
- ¼ cup plus 3 tablespoons sugar
- 2 tablespoons port wine
- 2 pinches of cream of tartar
- 1 cup heavy cream
- ½ tablespoon unflavored gelatin

FOR GARNISH
- chocolate leaves and cocoa

INGREDIENT TIP
You can add 2 tablespoons coffee to the dark mousse and 2 tablespoons orange juice to the white mousse.

1 Finely chop the semisweet and white chocolate. In a double boiler over low heat, combine 2 egg yolks, 2 tablespoons sugar, and 2 tablespoons water. Whisk for 5 minutes until thick. Whisk in the semisweet chocolate until melted. Stir in the port.

2 In a clean double boiler over low heat, beat 2 egg whites, pinch cream of tartar, 2 tablespoons sugar, and 1 teaspoon water with a mixer until stiff, about 4 minutes. Beat ½ cup cream until just stiff. Fold the whipped cream, then the whites into the chocolate. Scrape into an 8-inch springform or soufflé dish. Chill for 2 hours.

3 Sprinkle the gelatin over 2 tablespoons water; set aside. In a double boiler, whisk the 2 remaining yolks, 2 tablespoons *each* sugar and water as above (Step 1). Stir in the white chocolate, then the gelatin.

4 Beat the remaining 2 egg whites, 1 tablespoon sugar, and pinch cream of tartar in a double boiler; beat the remaining ½ cup cream as above (Step 2). Fold the whipped cream and whites into the white chocolate. Spread over the dark mousse. Cover; chill for 2 hours. Slice the mousse and garnish.

Step 1

Step 3

Step 4

Preparation: 35 minutes
Chilling: 4 hours
Per serving: 333 cal; 6 g pro;
22 g fat; 30 g carb.

TYPICALLY BRITISH
Three hundred years ago, chocolate houses were the rage in London among the wealthy. These establishments offered chocolate in beverage form only—the "eating" kind had not yet been invented. The British love for cocoa and chocolate continues to this day.

COOKING TIP

Here's how to make pretty chocolate leaves for garnishing the mousse. Take (untreated) real leaves—laurel or rose, for example—and thickly brush the underside with melted chocolate. Set aside until dried, then carefully peel off the green leaves.

SERVING TIP

Make this dessert extra-special by decorating each portion with chocolate leaves, grated or shaved chocolate, or fine store-bought candies.

SERVING TIPS Sip fragrant currant tea or a dark golden semidry sherry, such as Amontillado, with this scrumptious trifle. Create fanciful decorations of whipped cream using a pastry bag.

HEAVENLY CHOCOLATE TRIFLE

GREAT BRITAIN

INGREDIENTS
(Serves 8)

FOR THE CAKE
- 5 large eggs
- ½ cup sugar
- 1 teaspoon vanilla extract
- ¾ cup cake flour
- ⅓ cup cocoa powder
- 4 tablespoons butter, melted

FOR THE CUSTARD
- 2 cups milk
- 4 large egg yolks
- ⅔ cup sugar
- 3 tablespoons cornstarch
- 1 teaspoon vanilla extract
- 1 cup heavy cream

IN ADDITION
- 1½ cups red currants
- ⅓ cup sweet sherry
- ½ cup raspberry jam
- 8 thin chocolate wafers

INGREDIENT TIP
If you can't find red currants, use red raspberries.

In this particularly luxuriant creation from the British Isles, a delicate sherry cream is exquisitely combined with a light chocolate cake and red currants or fresh raspberries.

1 Preheat the oven to 350°F. Beat the eggs, sugar, vanilla, and 2 tablespoons hot water with an electric mixer for 5 minutes, until thick and pale. Sift in the flour and cocoa and fold in gently. Fold in the butter. Pour the batter into a greased 9-inch pan and bake for 30 minutes. Let cool.

2 For the custard, in a saucepan, bring the milk to a boil. In a bowl, whisk the yolks and sugar until thick. Whisk in the cornstarch and some of the hot milk. Whisk this mixture into the remaining warm milk. Cook over low heat until thick, about 5 minutes. Transfer the custard to a bowl; stir in the vanilla. Refrigerate, covered, for 2 hours.

3 Beat the heavy cream until stiff. Fold two thirds of it into the custard. Wash the currants and strip off the stems with a fork. Cut the cake into 1-inch cubes. Put half the cubes in the serving bowl; drizzle with half the sherry and jam. Top with a quarter of the custard. Repeat layering once.

4 Sprinkle currants over the trifle; top with remaining custard. Refrigerate for 2 hours. Decorate with the remaining plain whipped cream and the chocolate wafers.

Step 1

Step 3

Step 4

Preparation: 50 minutes
Baking: 30 minutes
Chilling: 2 hours
Per serving: 528 cal; 10 g pro; 26 g fat; 65 g carb.

TYPICALLY ENGLISH
The English love the custardy, cake-and-fruit confections called trifles, which have been a part of their cuisine for centuries. Although jams are usually layered into this elaborate treat, English cooks will also use any ripe fruits available in the market.

$\mathscr{S}$TRAWBERRY-WHITE CHOCOLATE TERRINE

GREAT BRITAIN

INGREDIENTS
(Serves 6)

- 1½ tablespoons unflavored gelatin
- 4 ounces white chocolate
- ¾ cup plus 2 tablespoons milk
- ½ lemon
- 1 pint strawberries
- 2 tablespoons sugar
- 1 cup heavy cream

IN ADDITION

- ½ cup heavy cream
- 1 tablespoon sugar

INGREDIENT TIP

White chocolate scorches easily, so be careful to melt it gently over very low heat.

This pretty dessert—perfect for a buffet—takes less time to prepare than you think. White chocolate lends rich flavor and texture to the classic duo of fresh strawberries and cream.

1 Sprinkle the gelatin over ¼ cup water. Set aside for 5 minutes. Coarsely chop the white chocolate. Place in a small saucepan over low heat with the milk. Stir occasionally until melted and hot; transfer to a medium bowl. Whisk in the softened gelatin; reserve.

2 Finely grate the peel from the lemon, and squeeze the juice. Hull the strawberries and set aside ½ cup. Place the remaining berries in a food processor with the sugar, lemon juice, and grated peel. Stir into the white chocolate.

3 Beat 1 cup heavy cream just until stiff. Fold into the white chocolate. Scrape the mixture into a 5-cup terrine mold and refrigerate for at least 3 hours, until set.

4 To serve, unmold the terrine onto a serving plate. Beat the remaining ½ cup heavy cream and 1 tablespoon sugar until stiff. Slice the reserved berries. Pipe the cream decoratively on the terrine and garnish with the strawberry slices.

Step 2

Step 4

Step 4

Preparation: 35 minutes
Chilling: 3 hours
Per serving: 370 cal; 5 g pro;
29 g fat, 24 g carb.

TYPICALLY CAMBRIDGE
Along the Cam River and in the green regions around the university town of Cambridge, England, sweet juicy strawberries appear each spring. The local harvest is enjoyed fresh and whole—or in sweet tart desserts like this sumptuous terrine.

COOKING TIP

For this terrine, use an oblong ring or rectangular mold. To make unmolding easier, cover with a warm towel, then place a serving platter upside down on the mold and turn both over. Or line the interior with dampened plastic wrap before pouring in the cream (the damp wrap will stick to the mold).

SERVING TIPS

The terrine can also be served frozen or partially frozen. For an accompaniment, a kiwi sauce is wonderful. Simply puree peeled kiwis with a bit of sugar and lemon juice.

LEMON-BERRY MERINGUES

SWEDEN

These sweet, delicate meringues, sandwiched with a fruity lemon filling and crowned with fresh berries, are splendid summertime desserts. They're elegant yet easy to make.

INGREDIENTS

(Serves 4)

- 2 egg whites
- ¾ cup confectioners' sugar plus additional for dusting
- ⅔ cup milk
- 2 egg yolks
- 3 tablespoons granulated sugar
- 1 tablespoon plus 1½ teaspoons all-purpose flour
- pinch of salt
- ½ teaspoon grated lemon peel
- ½ cup heavy cream
- fresh raspberries and blackberries
- mint leaves or lemon balm (optional)

INGREDIENT TIPS

- For the greatest volume of meringue, use the egg whites at room temperature.
- You can also use blueberries, small strawberries, and red or black currants.

1 In a large bowl over a saucepan of hot water, briskly whisk the egg whites with ¾ cup confectioners' sugar until stiff.

Step 1

2 Preheat the oven to 200°F. With a pencil, mark eight 2½-inch rounds on a sheet of parchment or wax paper. Place the paper marked side down on a baking sheet. Spoon the meringue into a pastry bag fitted with a ¼-inch plain tip and pipe out the meringue in a spiral to fill the circle outlines, starting from the center. Bake for 1¼–1½ hours with the oven door slightly open.

Step 2

3 Heat the milk to boiling in a small saucepan. In a medium bowl, whisk the yolks, granulated sugar, flour, and salt until smooth and whisk in one third of the hot milk. Pour into the milk in the pan and cook over medium heat, stirring, for 5 minutes, until thickened. Stir in the lemon peel. Transfer to a bowl and refrigerate until cold.

4 No more than 30 minutes before serving, spread the lemon filling over 4 meringues. Top with the remaining meringues. Beat the heavy cream until stiff and pipe onto the meringues. Garnish with the berries and mint. Dust with confectioners' sugar.

Step 4

Preparation: 35 minutes
Cooking: 1¼–1½ hours
Per serving: 251 cal; 3 g pro; 11 g fat; 37 g carb.

TYPICALLY SWEDISH

When the days are long and the nights are short during solstice-time in Sweden, children and adults alike celebrate with midsummer night parties. These are occasions for feasting on warm and cold dishes and desserts, such as these sweet creams with fresh berries.

COOKING TIP

For the meringues, set the oven on the lowest heat level—they're actually dried out rather than baked. The surface should remain light-colored. Keep the oven door slightly open with a wooden spoon handle so the moisture can escape. Unfilled meringues can be stored in airtight containers for about three weeks.

SERVING TIP

Offer a thirst quencher made from berry syrup: Just pour ice-cold water or club soda into a little of the syrup and decorate with a slice of lemon.

APPLE CHARLOTTE RUSSE

RUSSIA

It's hard to resist indulging immediately in this velvety cheesecake with its thick wreath of light ladyfingers. But don't be tempted—the charlotte needs several hours to chill!

INGREDIENTS
(Serves 8)

- 3 small tart apples, such as Granny Smith
- 2 tablespoons lemon juice
- ½ cup sugar
- 1 package unflavored gelatin
- 2 large egg yolks
- ½ cup apple juice
- 1 pound cream cheese, softened
- 3 ounces crisp ladyfingers
- 1½ cups heavy cream

IN ADDITION
- 1 red apple, cut in wedges
- 2 teaspoons lemon juice

INGREDIENT TIP
During the autumn months, you can use tart apples, such as Cortland, Gravenstein, Greening, and Northern Spy.

1 Peel, core, and finely dice the tart apples. Place in a saucepan with 2 tablespoons *each* lemon juice and sugar; simmer for 5 minutes until crisp-tender. Let cool.

2 Sprinkle the gelatin over ¼ cup water. In a double boiler over simmering water, whisk the yolks, apple juice, and remaining 6 tablespoons sugar until hot and thick, 4–5 minutes. Stir in the gelatin.

3 Whisk in the cream cheese, then the cooked apples until blended. Refrigerate for 10 minutes, until beginning to gel. Meanwhile, lightly grease an 8-inch spring-form pan. Split the ladyfingers, then stand the cookies around the wall of the pan.

4 Beat 1 cup of the cream until stiff; fold into the apple-cheese mixture. Scrape into the pan. Cover and chill for 3 hours.

5 To serve, beat the remaining ½ cup cream. Sprinkle the apple wedges with the lemon juice. Carefully open the spring-form and decorate the charlotte with rosettes of whipped cream and apple wedges.

Step 1

Step 1

Step 3

Preparation: 40 minutes
Chilling: 3 hours
Per serving: 497 cal; 8 g pro; 39 g fat; 32 g carb.

TYPICALLY RUSSIAN
The charlotte russe was invented in the early 19th century by the renowned French chef and culinary scholar Antonin Carême at the court of Czar Alexander I in St. Petersburg. In the meantime, confectioners have developed many variations for this sumptuous dessert.

COOKING TIPS

• Very carefully halve the ladyfingers lengthwise, using a serrated knife so they don't crumble.
• To get the charlotte out of the pan intact, carefully loosen the sides of the cake with a sharp knife before releasing the springform.

SERVING TIP

Try apple tea with this dessert. For 8 servings, pour about 6 cups of boiling water and 2 cups hot sweet cider or apple juice over 4 tablespoons black tea. Add a dash of cinnamon and brew for about 4 minutes. Strain into a teapot and serve.

CREAM PUFFS—THREE WAYS

For an exquisite ending to a special meal, try these little pastries with a tangy strawberry, silky chocolate, or mixed-berry filling.

BASIC PASTRY RECIPE

(18 CREAM PUFFS)
- 3 tablespoons butter
- salt
- ½ cup flour
- 2 large eggs

IN ADDITION
- wax paper

You can bake the pastries up to two days ahead. Store airtight at room temperature, then just fill and serve.

1 Preheat the oven to 425°F. Line 1 or 2 large baking sheets with wax or parchment paper. Set aside.

2 For the batter, bring ½ cup water with the butter and a pinch of salt to a boil in a saucepan. Add the flour and stir until the dough forms a mass that comes away from the pan. Remove from the heat and beat in the eggs one at a time.

3 Put the dough into a pastry bag with a star-shaped tip and pipe out 18 one-inch balls onto the baking paper, evenly spaced apart. Bake for about 25 minutes, until crisp and browned. Immediately slice open with a knife and let cool.

SILKY STRAWBERRY

Preparation: 30 minutes   Baking: 25 minutes

GERMANY

FOR THE FILLING
- ¼ pint strawberries
- 2 tablespoons orange liqueur
- 4 ounces cream cheese, softened
- ¼ cup confectioners' sugar, plus more for dusting
- ½ cup heavy cream

4 Slice the berries and mix with the liqueur; let rest for 30 minutes. Stir in the cream cheese and sugar. Whip the cream and fold it in.

5 Fill cream puffs with the strawberry mixture and dust with confectioners' sugar.

MIXED BERRY

Preparation: 30 minutes   Baking: 25 minutes

SWEDEN

FOR THE FILLING
- ½ cup berries
- 1 tablespoon sugar
- ⅔ cup heavy cream
- ½ cup confectioners' sugar
- 2 tablespoons lemon juice

4 Wash the berries, pat dry, and mix with the sugar. Set aside for 10 minutes.

5 Beat the cream until stiff. Fold in the sugared berries. Fill the cream puffs with the berry cream.

6 In a small bowl, stir the confectioners' sugar and lemon juice until smooth. Brush it over the cream puffs as a glaze.

CHOCOLATE MOUSSE

Preparation: 30 minutes   Baking: 25 minutes

FRANCE

FOR THE FILLING
- 1 ounce semisweet chocolate
- 1 cup heavy cream
- ¼ cup confectioners' sugar
- 2 tablespoons cocoa powder

4 Chop the chocolate; melt it in a double boiler or the microwave.

5 Whip the heavy cream until stiff. Sift in the confectioners' sugar and cocoa powder and whisk until smooth.

6 Fill cream puffs with the chocolate cream. Transfer the melted chocolate to a small plastic bag and snip a tiny hole in a corner. Pipe chocolate over cream puffs in thin lines.

FRAGRANT MANGO DELIGHT

INDIA

INGREDIENTS
(Serves 4)

- 1 package unflavored gelatin
- 2 large, ripe mangos
- ¾ cup buttermilk
- ¼ cup sugar
- 2 teaspoons lemon juice
- 1 teaspoon vanilla extract
- ½ cup heavy cream
- 1 kiwi
- ¼ cup grated coconut

INGREDIENT TIP

Mangos taste good only when fully ripe. They should respond easily to light finger pressure and give off a strong sweet aroma.

Here's something refreshing for the health-conscious gourmet: a buttermilk-based, tangy-sweet mango mousse served with fresh fruit and a sprinkling of toasted grated coconut.

1 Place the gelatin in a small saucepan with ¼ cup cold water; let sit for about 5 minutes. Peel 1 mango. Cut the pulp from the pit with a sharp knife and puree in a blender or food processor with the buttermilk, sugar, lemon juice, and vanilla.

2 Place the gelatin over low heat to dissolve. Stir it into the mango puree. Refrigerate the puree until it starts to gel.

3 In a medium bowl, beat the cream until stiff and fold in the mango puree with a rubber spatula until no streaks of cream remain. Cover and refrigerate for 2 hours, until the mousse is firm.

4 To serve, peel the remaining mango and cut the pulp from the pit in slices. Peel the kiwi and slice into wedges. Toast the coconut in a small dry skillet.

5 Scoop the mousse onto plates or dessert dishes with the mango and kiwi slices. Sprinkle with the toasted coconut.

Step 1

Step 4

Step 4

Preparation: 35 minutes
Chilling: 2 hours
Per serving: 296 cal; 5 g pro; 13 g fat; 43 g carb.

TYPICALLY INDIAN
The mango tree originated in tropical East and Southeast Asia. In India, the aromatic fruit has been cultivated for millennia, and is as popular there as the apple is here.

COOKING TIPS

- Ripe mangos are sensitive to the cold and should not be stored in the refrigerator.
- Mango juice may stain kitchen towels and clothing, so be careful when peeling and preparing the fruit.

SERVING TIPS

Offer this treat as a fresh conclusion to a meal of spicy curry. Serve it with a cooling lassi, an Indian yogurt drink sometimes blended with fruit. Masala tea, spiced with cardamom, cinnamon, and cloves, is another traditional favorite.

$\mathscr{W}$HIPPED BANANA CREAM

BRAZIL

This sweet confection of banana puree, brown sugar, and whipped cream is quick and easy to prepare. A trio of spices give the dessert its incomparable flavor.

INGREDIENTS
(Serves 4)

- 1 lime
- 2 very ripe bananas
- 2 tablespoons brown sugar
- ½ teaspoon vanilla extract
- pinch of ground ginger
- pinch of ground cloves
- pinch of cinnamon
- ⅔ cup heavy cream

IN ADDITION

- 1 firm ripe banana
- 1 tablespoon cocoa powder

INGREDIENT TIP

You can use vanilla sugar in place of the vanilla extract. Or use the scraped-out seeds of a vanilla bean.

1 Finely grate the peel of the lime and squeeze the juice. Reserve 2 tablespoons of the juice.

Step 1

2 Peel the soft bananas and thoroughly mash them with an electric mixer, fork or hand blender. Immediately mix in the sugar, lime peel, and all but the reserved lime juice. Stir in the vanilla, ginger, cloves, and cinnamon.

Step 2

3 Beat the heavy cream until stiff, then fold lightly but thoroughly with a whisk or rubber spatula into the banana.

4 Peel the banana for the garnish and halve once crosswise and once lengthwise, so that there are 4 flat pieces. Make lengthwise cuts almost to the ends of these pieces so that a fan shape results, and sprinkle with the remaining lime juice.

Step 4

5 Distribute the banana cream among individual dessert plates. Lay a banana fan next to each portion. Dust with the cocoa powder and serve immediately.

Preparation: 30 minutes
Per serving: 250 cal; 2 g pro;
15 g fat; 29 g carb.

TYPICALLY BRAZILIAN
The banana was introduced to the Amazon from Africa by Portuguese traders. There are several varieties of the fruit, which Brazilian cooks use in both savory and sweet dishes. Banana desserts are often seasoned with cinnamon, clove, and vanilla.

COOKING TIPS

• This luscious cream tastes great chilled—and it's delicious semi-frozen (freeze for about 1 hour).

• Prepare the banana fans just before serving so that the fruit will not discolor.

SERVING TIP

Instead of making the banana fans, you can garnish the dessert with long, skinny strips of lime zest.

CARIBBEAN PINEAPPLE CHIFFON

MARTINIQUE

INGREDIENTS
(Serves 4)

FOR THE MOUSSE
- 1 ripe pineapple
- ½ cup light brown sugar
- 2½ tablespoons cornstarch
- 2 tablespoons dark rum
- ½ teaspoon vanilla extract
- 3 large eggs, separated
- 3 tablespoons granulated sugar
- pinch of cream of tartar

IN ADDITION
- ½ cup confectioners' sugar
- ½ cup heavy cream
- 1 teaspoon vanilla extract
- berries for garnish

INGREDIENT TIP

When you're shopping for fresh pineapple, rely on your nose. If the base of the fruit smells sweet, it's ripe.

From the sultry Caribbean comes this mouthwatering dessert. It's served with a rich vanilla cream sauce on the side and a sprinkling of bright, fresh raspberries.

1 Peel and trim the pineapple. Cut 4 thin slices and set aside. Quarter the rest; remove the core. Cube the pineapple, place in a saucepan with the brown sugar, and bring to a boil. Mix 2 tablespoons cornstarch with 2 tablespoons water. Add to the pan and bring to a boil. Add the rum and vanilla and and let cool. Puree the mixture and strain.

Step 1

2 Place the egg whites, granulated sugar, cream of tartar, and 1 tablespoon water in a double boiler over simmering water. Stir with a rubber spatula until the whites reach 160°F. Remove from heat; beat until stiff. Mix the remaining cornstarch with 3 tablespoons water; let sit for 1 minute. Bring to a boil, stirring. Let cool and whisk into the whites. Fold the pineapple puree into the whites, a third at a time. Refrigerate for 2 hours.

Step 1

3 Beat the egg yolks and confectioners' sugar in a double boiler for 3 minutes. Gradually stir in the cream; cook for 3 minutes longer, until thick. Remove from the heat and stir in the vanilla. Beat until cool.

Step 2

4 Divide the pineapple chiffon into bowls. Garnish with the pineapple slices and berries. Serve with the vanilla custard sauce.

Preparation: 1 hour
Chilling: 2 hours
Per serving: 527 cal; 6 g pro; 16 g fat; 90 g carb.

TYPICALLY MARTINIQUE
Contrary to popular belief, pineapples grow on the ground—not on trees! These tangy fruits originated in South America but are now cultivated in other tropical regions. In Martinique, the fresh crop is enjoyed in exquisite dishes, such as this airy dessert.

COOKING TIPS

• When stirring the egg whites over the simmering water, take care to stir around the edges and bottom of the pan so that the whites don't cook.

  You don't need a candy thermometer for the whites; a meat thermometer will work just as well.

SERVING TIPS

Offer this dessert after a meal from the grill. For an ideal beverage, make a cocktail of pineapple and orange juices with a dash of coconut liqueur and white rum. Garnish with pineapple and serve with a straw.

S E R V I N G   T I P Instead of using ice cream dishes, remove the hard central core from 6 pineapple slices and lay them on dessert plates. Put a scoop of the coconut ice cream in the center.

50

COCO-LIME SUNDAES

BARBADOS

It's an exotic surprise for your summer party—smooth coconut ice cream drizzled with a sweet-sour lime syrup. The ice-cold dessert can be prepared well in advance.

INGREDIENTS
(Serves 6)

- 1 vanilla bean
- 1 cup heavy cream
- 5 tablespoons sugar
- salt
- 1 can (13½ ounces) unsweetened coconut milk
- ½ cup crème fraîche or sour cream

FOR THE SYRUP
- 2 limes
- ½ cup sugar

IN ADDITION
- ½ cup heavy cream

INGREDIENT TIPS
- Canned coconut milk is available at Asian markets.
- If limes are unavailable, simply prepare the syrup with lemons.

1 Split the vanilla bean lengthwise and scrape out the pulp. Put the pulp, bean, heavy cream, sugar, and a pinch of salt into a saucepan and stir it over low heat until the sugar is melted. Remove from the heat and let cool.

2 Remove the vanilla bean from the cream. Stir in the coconut milk and crème fraîche. Cover and refrigerate the mixture for at least 1 hour. Freeze in an ice cream maker according to the manufacturer's instructions.

3 Meanwhile, wash the limes with hot water and dry. Strip off the peel with a zester. Squeeze out the lime juice.

4 Put the lime juice, peel, sugar, and ½ cup water in a saucepan and simmer for about 10 minutes. Let cool.

5 Beat the heavy cream until stiff. Scoop the ice cream into serving dishes. Drizzle the lime syrup over the ice cream, then garnish with some of the whipped cream. Serve immediately.

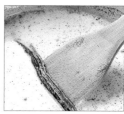

Step 1

Step 2

Step 3

Preparation: 30 minutes
Chilling: 1 hour
Per serving: 512 cal; 3 g pro; 43 g fat; 32 g carb.

TYPICALLY BARBADOS
The lime probably originated in Central Asia or the subcontinent, but today it is planted in nearly all tropical regions. In the Caribbean, its juice and bitter peel are popular, refreshing ingredients for sweet and hearty dishes as well as mixed drinks.

CHERRY PAVLOVA

From Down Under comes this delight for the eyes and taste buds—a sumptuous mix of cherries and cream artistically layered onto a light, crisp round of meringue.

INGREDIENTS

(Serves 8)

FOR THE MERINGUE

- 3 large egg whites
- salt
- ⅓ cup granulated sugar
- ⅔ cup confectioners' sugar
- 1 tablespoon cornstarch

FOR THE FILLING

- ½ pint sour cherries
- ½ pint sweet cherries
- 3 tablespoons granulated sugar
- 1 cup heavy cream
- 1 teaspoon vanilla extract

IN ADDITION

- wax or parchment paper

INGREDIENT TIP

If you can find only one kind of cherry, use twice the quantity called for here and sweeten to taste. When cherries are out of season, pitted sour cherries from a can are the best substitute.

1 Preheat the oven to 200°F. Beat the egg whites and a pinch of salt in a bowl until foamy; gradually add the granulated sugar and continue beating until stiff. Sift the confectioners' sugar and cornstarch over the egg whites and carefully fold in.

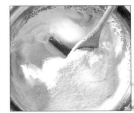

Step 1

2 Draw a 7-inch circle on a sheet of wax or parchment paper and place the paper on a baking sheet with marked side down.

3 Spoon the egg whites into a pastry bag with a star tip. Pipe half of the meringue onto the drawn circle to make a big, thick, outer rim. Pipe the rest of the meringue onto the paper to fill in the circle. Bake the meringue for 2 hours, until crisp and dry. Transfer to a wire rack to cool completely.

Step 3

4 Wash, stem, and pit the cherries. Reserve the sweet cherries. Bring the sour cherries to a boil with the sugar and 2 tablespoons water, then let cool.

5 Whip the cream and vanilla until stiff. Layer the cream with the sweet and sour cherries over the meringue to form a dome.

Step 4

Preparation: 35 minutes
Baking: 2 hours
Per serving: 221 cal; 2 g pro; 11 g fat; 29 g carb.

TYPICALLY AUSTRALIAN

This dessert, named for the Russian ballerina Anna Pavlova, probably originated during the dancer's visit to Australia in 1926. Legend has it that a Perth hotel cook was asked to create a special sweet for afternoon tea. Its form wa to be reminiscent of an ethereal ballet skirt.

COOKING TIPS

• Serve the Cherry Pavlova immediately after topping it so the meringue doesn't get too soft.

• As a variation, fold the pulp of 4 passion fruits and kiwi slices into the cream.

SERVING TIPS

Try this fluffy dessert after a meal of lamb chops with tender beans and carrots in butter. A coffee, mocha, or espresso should not be missing from the dessert course.

$\mathscr{N}$O-BAKE PEACH CHEESECAKE

USA

It's a snap to make this enchanting dessert, which features a mousselike filling of creamy cheese and peach puree atop a scrumptious cookie-crumb crust.

INGREDIENTS
(Serves 12)

- 6 ounces butter cookies
- 2 tablespoons granulated sugar
- ½ teaspoon cinnamon
- 4 tablespoons butter, melted

FOR THE MOUSSE
- 3 teaspoons unflavored gelatin
- 1 small lemon
- 1 can (28 ounces) peaches
- 1 pound cream cheese, softened
- ⅓ cup confectioners' sugar
- salt
- 1 cup heavy cream

IN ADDITION
- 1 can (28 ounces) peaches

INGREDIENT TIPS

- Fresh or canned apricots are also great in this dessert.
- Lower-fat Neufchâtel cream cheese also works here.

1 Place the cookies in a plastic bag and crush with a rolling pin. Mix in a bowl with the granulated sugar, cinnamon, and melted butter. Spread evenly over the bottom of a 10-inch springform cake pan and press down solidly. Refrigerate for 1 hour.

2 For the mousse, place the gelatin in a small saucepan with 3 tablespoons cold water; let sit for 5 minutes. Place the saucepan over low heat and stir the mixture until the gelatin dissolves.

3 Wash and dry the lemon, then finely grate the peel and squeeze out the juice. Strain the peaches and puree them with a blender or in a food processor. Add the lemon juice, grated lemon peel, dissolved gelatin, cream cheese, confectioners' sugar, and a pinch of salt. Pulse or blend until the mixture is smooth. Beat the cream until stiff. Gently fold it into the peach mixture.

4 Drain the second can of peaches and thinly slice. Lay half the sliced peaches over the cookie crust. Cover with the peach mixture and refrigerate for at least 3 hours. Decorate with the remaining peach slices.

Step 1

Step 3

Step 4

Preparation: 15 minutes
Chilling: 4 hours
Per serving: 378 cal; 5 g pro; 27 g fat; 31 g carb.

TYPICALLY CALIFORNIAN
In sun-drenched California, peaches grow especially well and develop a pronounced aroma. The state's vast orchards supply canners with the juicy summer fruits. Most canned peaches, in fact, are from California.

COOKING TIP

If you're using fresh peaches, you'll need about 2¼ pounds. Place the peaches briefly in boiling water, rinse in cold water, and strip off the skin with a knife. Hard fruits should be boiled for a few minutes longer. Halve the peaches, remove the pits, and continue with the recipe at left.

SERVING TIP

A coffee frappe makes an ideal refreshment. Brew some coffee with vanilla extract, lemon peel, and cinnamon. Strain, let cool, then freeze in an ice-cube tray. Crush the coffee cubes in a blender or food processor, spoon into glasses, and top with whipped cream.

SERVING TIP Frozen chocolate soufflé makes a wonderfully icy treat. Freeze the whole mold, loosely covered with foil, for at least 4 hours and up to 2 weeks, then garnish just before serving.

CHOCOLATE-WHISKEY SOUFFLÉ

USA

Semisweet chocolate and fine Southern whiskey give this silky cream dessert a nuanced flavor. It's a refrigerated soufflé, served cold and dressed up with chocolate shavings.

INGREDIENTS
(Serves 8)

- 7½ ounces semisweet chocolate
- 2 large eggs plus 2 large egg whites
- 4 tablespoons sugar
- 7 tablespoons Tennessee whiskey or bourbon
- 1 package unflavored gelatin
- pinch of cream of tartar
- 1¾ cups heavy cream

IN ADDITION
- Grated white chocolate as a garnish

INGREDIENT TIP

If you like, make the soufflé with bittersweet chocolate instead of the semisweet variety. The former contains more chocolate liquor, providing an intense flavor.

1 Shave ½ ounce of the chocolate into thin flakes. Set aside. Chop the remaining chocolate and melt in a double boiler set over simmering water. Let cool.

2 Separate the eggs and place the yolks in a clean double boiler set over simmering water. Whisk them with 2 tablespoons sugar for 4 minutes, until light and thick. Remove from the heat and whisk in the whiskey and melted chocolate.

3 In a small saucepan, soften the gelatin with ¼ cup cold water for 5 minutes. Place over low heat and stir the gelatin until dissolved. Stir into the chocolate mixture.

4 In a clean double boiler set over simmering water, beat the egg whites with the remaining sugar, 2 tablespoons water, and cream of tartar for 5–7 minutes, until stiff. Whip the cream. Fold the egg whites and cream into the chocolate mixture.

5 Form a foil collar around a 1-quart soufflé mold. Pour the chocolate into the mold and refrigerate for at least 3 hours. Remove the collar, then garnish with the white and semisweet chocolate shavings.

Step 1

Step 4

Step 5

Preparation: 50 minutes
Chilling: 3 hours
Per serving: 387 cal; 5 g pro; 28 g fat; 25 g carb.

TYPICALLY TENNESSEE
Tennessee is famous for its rich, full-bodied, amber-hued whiskey. Distilled from at least 51 percent grain, usually corn, it's a bourbon-type brew that's treated with maple-wood charcoal to intensify the flavor, then aged in charred oak barrels for about six years.

$\mathscr{B}$AKED ALASKA

USA

This dessert extravaganza is frozen on the inside, hot on the outside. A sumptuous cake base supports a filling of vanilla ice cream and raspberries and a thick covering of crisp meringue.

INGREDIENTS

(Serves 4)

FOR THE CAKE

- 3 tablespoons butter
- 2 tablespoons sugar
- 1 large egg
- 1 large egg yolk
- ⅔ cup flour
- 1 teaspoon baking powder
- 1 cup raspberries

FOR THE FILLING

- 1 cup vanilla ice cream

FOR THE MERINGUE

- 2 egg whites
- salt
- ¼ cup sugar

INGREDIENT TIP

You can use either fresh or frozen raspberries here. Simply thaw the frozen berries in the refrigerator.

1 Preheat the oven to 400°F. Grease an 8-inch springform pan. Beat the butter and sugar until light and fluffy. Add the egg and egg yolk and beat until smooth. In a small bowl, mix together the flour and baking powder and beat into the batter.

2 Spread the batter evenly in the pan. Distribute ¼ cup of the raspberries over it; bake for about 25 minutes. Let cool in the pan on a wire rack. Remove the cake from the pan. Place on a foil-lined baking sheet.

Step 2

3 Shortly before serving, heat the oven to 450°F. Cut the vanilla ice cream into coarse cubes and mound it over the cake with the remaining raspberries.

Step 3

4 Beat the egg whites with a pinch of salt until foamy. Continue beating the whites, gradually adding the sugar, until stiff. Spread the meringue over the cake, using the back of a spoon to make decorative peaks. Be sure to seal the cake edge with meringue.

5 Place the cake in the middle of the oven and bake for about 3 minutes, until the meringue peaks turn golden brown. Serve immediately.

Step 4

Preparation: 45 minutes
Cooking: 30 minutes
Per serving: 349 cal; 8 g pro;
15 g fat; 47 g carb.

TYPICALLY AMERICAN

Like a glacier or a snow-capped mountain, the Baked Alaska graces the table. An early version of the piping hot meringue-topped ice cream dessert—dubbed "Alaska-Florida"—was created at Delmonico's restaurant in New York City in the 19th century.

COOKING TIP

The cake should be completely cool before topping it with the ice cream and berries. If you like, prepare the cake a day in advance; let it cool, wrap in plastic, and refrigerate.

SERVING TIP

Offer a sugared berry mixture with this dessert: Combine ⅔ pint fresh or frozen berries (such as strawberries, blackberries, raspberries, and blueberries) and sweeten to taste. Tea or coffee go best with this cake.

KITCHEN GLOSSARY

The following explanations of ingredients and cooking techniques will help assure the success of these creamy desserts.

CRÈME FRAÎCHE
A tangy, very rich thickened cream with a fat content of at least 30 percent. This specialty of France is ideal for cooking because it won't curdle. It's also a sublime topping for fresh fruit, tarts, cobblers, and puddings.

EGGS
Unless otherwise specified, large is the assumed size of eggs in the recipes. Beaten egg white is made more solid with a dash of salt, sugar, or cream of tartar. When whipping egg whites, use eggs that are at least a few days old—you'll get greater volume than with just-purchased eggs.

ESPRESSO
As an ingredient in desserts, this strong, dark Italian roast adds a robust taste.

GELATIN
Unsweetened commercial granulated gelatin comes in ¼-ounce envelopes. Generally, 1 envelope will gel 2 cups of liquid. Always soak gelatin in cold water for a few minutes before dissolving it.

HEAVY CREAM
Cream with a fat content of 32 to 40 percent. It will double in volume when whipped.

ICE CREAM MAKERS
With these terrific appliances, which are available in manual and electric versions, you can create treats like the Caribbean-style coconut ice cream featured in our Coco-Lime Sundaes (see recipe, page 50). The manual ice cream makers are charmingly old-fashioned, with wooden buckets and hand-operated cranks, while the easy-to-use electric machines come conveniently equipped with motors that mimic this motion.

A CHOCOLATE PRIMER
Chocolate is one of the most invaluable ingredients in dessert recipes. Inside every cacao pod are some 20 to 50 cocoa beans, which undergo a process of fermentation, drying, roasting, grinding, and mixing to produce our favorite candy in all its forms.

Unsweetened chocolate
Also known as bitter, baking, or cooking chocolate, this variety is made from a mixture of cocoa butter and chocolate liquor, which is the (nonalcoholic) brown cocoa-bean paste that gives dark chocolate its defining color and taste.

Semisweet and bittersweet chocolates
These two popular varieties of chocolate consist of chocolate liquor blended with cocoa butter, sugar, and vanilla (bittersweet usually contains less sugar than semisweet).

Milk chocolate
Here, chocolate liquor is enhanced with dried or condensed milk to yield a milder confection.

White chocolate
Made of cocoa butter, dry milk, sugar, vanilla, and often lecithin. As it contains no chocolate liquor, it isn't considered "true" chocolate.

Cocoa powder
About 75 percent of the cocoa butter is removed from the roasted beans, leaving the chocolate liquor that's dried and ground to make this unsweetened powder.

LADYFINGERS

These small, tender oblongs of sponge cake are often soaked in liqueur or coffee and used in creamy desserts like tiramisu.

MASCARPONE CHEESE

This buttery cream cheese hails from Italy. Soft and thick, it's very popular in desserts.

MERINGUE

A mixture of stiffly beaten egg white and sugar. It can be used soft as a topping for pie, Baked Alaska, and other desserts. Or it can be dried in the oven to form a pastry with a dry surface and a chewy interior.

MOUSSE

Any of several molded desserts consisting of whipped cream or beaten egg whites combined with a sweetened custard, then chilled. Chocolate mousse is a shining example.

SUGAR

Granulated, confectioners', or brown sugar is used to sweeten nearly every delicious cream dessert. Brown sugar imparts a light molasses flavor. Be sure to

USEFUL UTENSILS

There are many small kitchen aids which help in preparing perfect creamy desserts.

Double boiler

Two pots that fit one inside the other; the lower pot holds simmering water. Delicate custards and puddings are gently cooked on the stovetop in a double-boiler.

Grater

This device, with its sharp-edged perforations, makes perfect shreds of chocolate, citrus peels, fresh coconut, nutmeg, and other primary dessert ingredients.

Molds

Whether metal, ceramic, or plastic, molds give foods a distinctive shape. Ice cream turns out better in the metal variety, as metal is the best conductor of cold.

Whisk

Many creamy desserts are made light and fluffy with egg whites or cream whipped into shape with a whisk.

Parchment or wax paper

Fragile pastry is easy to remove from this coated paper. Even meringues can be removed without breaking.

Pastry bags and tips

These fabric or plastic pastry bags with different tips are indispensable for those who like to decorate their desserts. They're used to apply whipped creams and frostings in creative designs—or to pipe out meringue.

Water bath

A pan or dish of food is set inside a larger pan of warm or hot water for gentle cooking in the oven.

store sugar in a dry place so it doesn't become lumpy.

VANILLA

Genuine vanilla has a wonderful, intense aroma. It's available in a few forms, including whole bean and liquid extract. When the whole bean is used, it's usually split lengthwise; the seeds are scraped into the dish that's being flavored. You can also add a bean to an airtight container of sugar to make vanilla sugar (use as you would plain sugar).

MENU SUGGESTIONS

Here are some enticing menu ideas from around the world to accompany the delicious desserts in this book. They're just right for when you want to surprise family or friends with an elegant meal. Or create your own special feasts using our suggestions as a starting point.

ITALY

TEMPTING TIRAMISU P. 6
Minestrone Soup
Steak alla Pizzaiola
—— ◆ ——

ICE CREAM BOMBE P. 8
Spinach-Stuffed Mushrooms
Fettuccine Alfredo
—— ◆ ——

LEMON-LIME CREAM P. 10
Arugula, Radicchio, and Endive Salad
Florentine Medallions of Pork
—— ◆ ——

PANNA COTTA WITH BLACKBERRY SAUCE P. 12
Sliced Mozzarella and Tomatoes
Saltimbocca alla Romana
—— ◆ ——

SWITZERLAND

FRUITED SWISS PARFAITS P. 16
Watercress and Potato Soup
Trout in Lemon Butter
—— ◆ ——

FRANCE

FLUFFY CHOCOLATE MOUSSE P. 18
Artichokes Vinaigrette
Chicken à la Provençale
—— ◆ ——

ALSATIAN RASPBERRY SOUFFLÉS P. 20
Puree of Pumpkin Soup
Poached Sole with Mushrooms
—— ◆ ——

CLASSIC CRÈME BRÛLÉE P. 22
Salad with Baked Goat Cheese
Steak with Red Wine and Shallots
—— ◆ ——

STRAWBERRY SWIRL P. 24
Clear Beef Bouillon
Roasted Chicken with Garlic
—— ◆ ——

GERMANY

RHUBARB-STRAWBERRY TREAT P. 26
Marinated Vegetables
Duck with Orange Sauce
—— ◆ ——

VANILLA BAVARIAN CREAM WITH RASPBERRY SAUCE P. 28
Ham and Cheese Quiche
Beef Stew with Carrots
—— ◆ ——

THE NETHERLANDS

DUTCH VANILLA DELIGHT P. 30
Split Pea Soup with Rye Croutons
Roasted Pork with Apples
—— ◆ ——

GREAT BRITAIN

BLACK-AND-WHITE MOUSSE CAKE P. 32
*Watercress and
Blue Cheese Salad
Salmon with Mustard Cream*

— ◆ —

HEAVENLY CHOCOLATE TRIFLE P. 34
*Shrimp Cocktail
Roast Beef with
Yorkshire Pudding*

— ◆ —

STRAWBERRY–WHITE CHOCOLATE TERRINE P. 36
*Mussels in Wine Sauce
Parslied Potatoes with
Lamb Chops*

— ◆ —

SWEDEN

LEMON-BERRY MERINGUES P. 38
*Smoked Salmon Toasts
Meatballs in
Cream Sauce*

— ◆ —

RUSSIA

APPLE CHARLOTTE RUSSE P. 40
*Red Beet Salad
with Sour Cream
Beef Stroganoff*

— ◆ —

INDIA

FRAGRANT MANGO DELIGHT P. 44
*Vegetable Fritters
Bengali Beef Curry*

— ◆ —

BRAZIL

WHIPPED BANANA CREAM P. 46
*Avocado Salad with
Palm Hearts
Shrimp in Coconut Milk*

— ◆ —

MARTINIQUE

CARIBBEAN PINEAPPLE CHIFFON P. 48
*Papaya with Ham
Spicy Fish Stew with Tomatoes*

— ◆ —

BARBADOS

COCO-LIME SUNDAES P. 50
*Fried Codfish Balls
Roasted Pork with Plantains*

— ◆ —

AUSTRALIA

CHERRY PAVLOVA P. 52
*Citrus Fruit Salad
Pappardelle with Ham*

— ◆ —

USA

NO-BAKE PEACH CHEESECAKE P. 54
*Classic Waldorf Salad
Cajun-Style Blackened Steaks*

— ◆ —

CHOCOLATE-WHISKEY SOUFFLÉ P. 56
*Corn and Shrimp Bisque
Lemon-Sauteed Chicken*

— ◆ —

BAKED ALASKA P. 58
*Tomato Soup
Salmon Steaks in Cucumber
Yogurt Sauce*

RECIPE INDEX

Photo Credits

Book cover and recipe photos:
©International Masters Publishers AB
Michael Brauner, Dorothee Gödert, Ansgar Pudens, Peter Rees,
Manuel Schnell

Agency Photos:
Introduction: Anzenberger: Giraudou page 5, bottom; Kraus pages 4, 5, center.
Focus: Kalvar page 5, top; F.M. Frei page 4, bottom.
White Star: Gumm page 4, top.
Photos for the "Typically" sections: AKG: page 52.
Anzenberger: T. Anzenberger pages 6, 51; Appelt page 56; Sieon page 46.
Bilderberg: Boisvieux page 44; Franke pages 12, 20; Grames page 48;
Horacek page 22. Das Fotoarchiv: Mayer page 35. Focus: Kluyver p. 38;
Snowdon/Hoyer page 24. F. M. Frei: page 8. IFA: TPL page 18.
Image Bank: Hartmann page 27. Kader: Juergen page 28.
Look: Heeb page 58; Martini page 11. Mauritius: Pascal page 54;
Thonig page 30; Waldkirch page 40. Studio X/Gamma: Sander page 32.
Visionbank: page 36. White Star: Reichelt page 16.